Lady Diva Boss™

This Notebook Belongs to:

_____

THE PERSON
THAT CAN
CHANGE YOUR
LIFE IS READING
THIS RIGHT
NOW.

Discipline

DISTRACTION

FEAR kills more **dreams** than **failure** ever could!

_____

_____

_____

_____

_____

_____

_____

_____

_____

_____

_____

_____

_____

_____

_____

_____

_____

_____

JUST REMEMBER,
YOU CAN'T
DEPOSIT
EXCUSES SIS!

You don't get better by chance, You get better by change.

Think in ink.

"Your past doesn't define you, it prepares you."

Success is not a straight line,

it zig zags.

FUTURE M.D.E.
MILLION DOLLAR EARNER

_____

_____

_____

_____

_____

_____

_____

_____

_____

_____

_____

_____

_____

_____

_____

_____

_____

_____

_____

There's a difference between a
full schedule and a fool schedule.
Which one is yours?

Am I working hard or hardly working?

_____

_____

_____

_____

_____

_____

_____

_____

_____

_____

_____

_____

_____

_____

_____

_____

_____

You are either
building your empire,
or you are building
someone else's.

WORKING ON MY MBA:
MILLION DOLLAR
BANK
ACCOUNT

_____
_____
_____
_____
_____
_____
_____
_____
_____
_____
_____
_____
_____
_____
_____
_____
_____
_____
_____
_____
_____
_____
_____

dream

---

*You can keep your comfort
or you can keep your dream.
You can't keep both.
-The Dream Giver*

_____

_____

_____

_____

_____

_____

_____

_____

_____

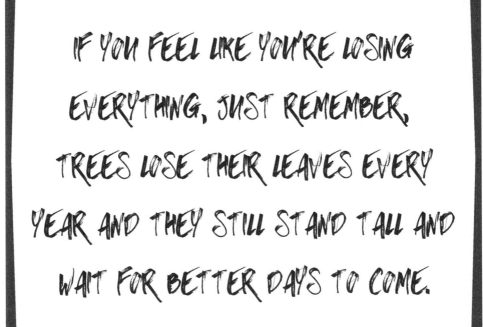

IF YOU FEEL LIKE YOU'RE LOSING EVERYTHING, JUST REMEMBER, TREES LOSE THEIR LEAVES EVERY YEAR AND THEY STILL STAND TALL AND WAIT FOR BETTER DAYS TO COME.

A Lady Diva Boss doesn't see with her eyes, she sees with her mind.

_____

_____

_____

_____

_____

_____

_____

_____

_____

_____

_____

_____

_____

_____

_____

_____

What we tolerate,
we give permission
to exist in our lives.

The greatest prison people live in is the fear of what other people think.

I can!
I will!
Watch me!

_____

_____

_____

_____

_____

_____

_____

_____

_____

HARD WORK DOESN'T SCARE A LADY DIVA BOSS, BUT AN AVERAGE AND ORDINARY LIFE DOES.

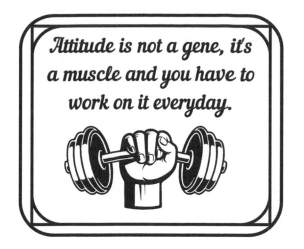

Attitude is not a gene, it's a muscle and you have to work on it everyday.

Sometimes, you have to let go of the good things, in order to make room for the great things.

Do it afraid!

_____

_____

_____

_____

_____

_____

_____

_____

_____

_____

_____

_____

_____

_____

_____

_____

_____

_____

NO PRESSURE
NO DIAMONDS.

Someone else out there needs you to get where you're supposed to be so they can win too!

It's better to take the long road to success and greatness, than to take the short road to failure and mediocrity.

THE RIGHT
PATH CROSSED
WITH THE
RIGHT PERSON
MAKES THE
RIGHT THINGS
HAPPEN.

_____

_____

_____

_____

_____

_____

_____

_____

_____

_____

_____

_____

_____

_____

_____

_____

_____

_____

_____

_____

_____

_____

Your success helps everyone and hurts no one. Your failure helps no one and hurts everyone.

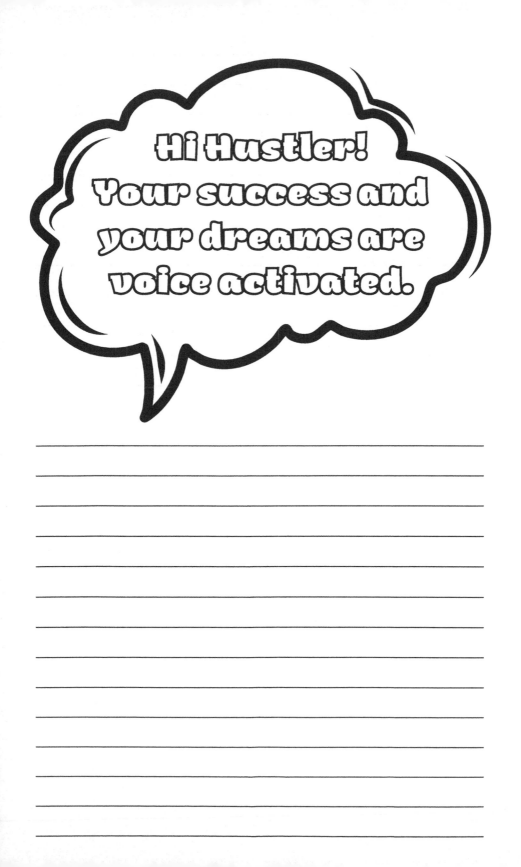

_____

_____

_____

_____

_____

_____

_____

_____

_____

_____

_____

_____

_____

_____

_____

_____

_____

_____

NOTE TO SELF:
YOU WILL NEVER OUTPERFORM
YOUR BELIEF LEVEL.

I am mission driven,
Not money driven.

Be a sellout!
Sell out to your own
dreams instead of
making someone
else's come true.

WE ARE NOT BORN WINNERS.
WE ARE NOT BORN LOSERS.
WE ARE BORN CHOOSERS.

You don't have time to wait on people that are waiting.

••●•• ♥ ••●••

SOMETIMES, IT'S NOT ABOUT KNOWING
WHAT YOU WANT, IT'S ABOUT KNOWING
WHAT YOU DON'T WANT.

If you aren't willing to sacrifice for what you want. what you want becomes the sacrifice.

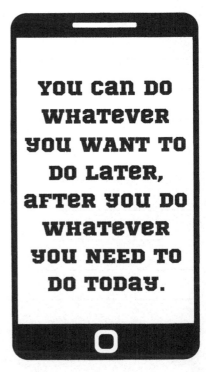

YOU CAN DO WHATEVER YOU WANT TO DO LATER, AFTER YOU DO WHATEVER YOU NEED TO DO TODAY.

Where you are right now is just temporary, it's where you are going that matters the most.

You can't do epic things with basic people.

Don't look for get rich quick,
look for get rich permanently.

YOU ARE GOING TO HAVE DISTRACTIONS WHETHER YOU'RE WINNING OR LOSING. YOU MIGHT AS WELL BE WINNING.

There's no
winning
when you
wait.

Thank you!

Reorder Here:

 https://www.amazon.com/author/ladydivaboss

We appreciate your 5 Star review!

Have a Team?
Ask about our customizations!

 bossbabe@ladydivaboss.com

Find us on Social Media

 https://www.facebook.com/groups/ladydivaboss

 @ladydivabossofficial

 www.ladydivaboss.com